Beauty of
Michigan

Beauty of
Michigan

Text: Louie Cook
Concept & Design: Robert D. Shangle

First Printing August, 1990
Published by LTA Publishing Company
2735 S.E. Raymond Street, Portland, Oregon 97202
Robert D. Shangle, Publisher

"Learn about America in a beautiful way."

Library of Congress Cataloging-in-Publication Data

Cook, Louis, 1915-

       p.   cm.

    Beauty of Michigan.

    ISBN 0-914343-81-5: 19.95. — ISBN 0-914343-80-7
(pbk.): $9.95

    1. Michigan — Description and travel — 1981 — Views.

    2. Michigan — Description and travel — 1981 — Guide-
books. I. Title.

F567.C65   1989   89-38292

917.7404'43 — dc20   CIP

Contents

Introduction   7

Names of Michigan   11

The Lowlands   13

The Uplands   65

The Highlands   70

The Valleys   73

Introduction

The look of Michigan has been vastly transformed in the last 150 years, and a good case can be made for the idea that civilization has improved it in many ways. The early settlers made little comment, however, on how things looked. They were immersed in clearing land, building railroads, and surviving.

The kind of painters who gave us immortal vistas of the Hudson River in early times do not seem to have been attracted to Michigan, where indeed there would have been few to buy their works.

But we know a great deal about the look of the land from an adventurous French politician and lawyer, Alexis de Tocqueville, who visited Michigan in the summer of 1831 and deliberately sought out the wildest, most inhospitable and most uncomfortable area he could reach on foot or horseback. People thought he was crazy.

In his "Journey to America" de Tocqueville described his arrival in Detroit at 4 p.m. on July 22 and looking up Father Gabriel Richard, a Catholic priest who published the city's first newspaper and was one of the founders of the University of Michigan. Father Richard's coffin still reposes in Ste. Anne's Church in Detroit.

A land speculator tried to tout de Tocqueville toward areas in the state already under development, warning him that in the direction of Pontiac and Saginaw lay "impenetrable forest which stretched endlessly to the northwest, where one finds only wild beasts and Indians." That was what de Tocqueville was looking for. Hiring a horse and shouldering his double-barreled percussion cap rifle — an object of curiosity and envy in those times — he set out toward Pontiac.

De Tocqueville found himself in deep forest a mile after leaving the Detroit River. That would have put him just past Grand Circus Park in present-day Detroit. He would have journeyed down dirt roads that became the site of skyscrapers, housing the financial center of Michigan.

He arrived in Pontiac after sundown: "Twenty very clean and very pretty houses . . . a transparent stream . . . and the everlasting forest all around." There were hotels in Pontiac — two, in fact — and the owner of the one de Tocqueville chose was incredulous when informed that the Frenchman intended to go to Saginaw.

"Do you know that Saginaw is the last inhabited point until you come to the Pacific Ocean? Do you know that from here you find hardly anything but wilds and untrod solitudes?" There was more, including reference to forest fever, a common and often fatal ailment among Michigan settlers who spent time in the damp and dark forest lands.

So de Tocqueville and a friend from France set out into the forest. His story of his experiences is an odd account, varying from poetic admiration of Michigan to abject terror.

Here's what he wrote following a canoe trip on the Saginaw River: ". . . a flowering solitude, delightful and scented; a magnificent dwelling, a living palace built for man . . . the serenity of universal calm reigned around us . . . we talked less and less and soon found we put our thought into whispers. Finally we fell silent and both of us fell into a tranquil reverie full of inexpressible charm."

And then: "At midday the sun darts its beams on the forest and one hears in its depths something like a long sigh, a plaintive cry lingering in the distance. It is the last stir of the dying wind. Then everything around you falls back into silence so deep, a stillness so complete that the soul is invaded by a kind of religious terror . . . the forest trees seem to form but one whole, immense and indestructible edifice under whose vaults eternal darkness reigns. On whatever side he looks, he sees nothing but a field of violence and destruction. Broken trees and torn trunks, everything testifies that the elements are here perpetually at war. All is still in the woods, all is silent under their leaves. One would say for a moment the Creator has turned his face away and all the forces of nature are paralyzed."

De Tocqueville's poetic insight into early Michigan and the people who inhabited various portions of it were all the more remarkable considering the distractions he encountered. Rattlesnakes abounded in the meadow grass along the streams, and then there were the mosquitoes: "By day they stopped us sketching, writing or staying one moment in the same place; by night they circled in their thousands around us . . . woken by the pain of their stings we covered our heads in the sheets, but their needles went through them . . . "

De Tocqueville made it back to Detroit safely, and took a steamer to Sault Ste. Marie, Bois Blanc, and Mackinac Islands and on to Green Bay, Wisconsin. His accounts of his further Michigan travels were mostly concerned with Indians met along the way. Nothing stirred him quite as much as his days and nights in the deep forest.

And the forest was unusual. It was part of the great hardwood forest of the Ohio basin and covered all of what is now Michigan, except for a few cleared areas in the southwest corner, probably the sites of Indian cornfields. On the dry gravel lands were red, black and white oaks, hickory, ash, cherry, basswood, and walnut. In the lowlands grew maple, elm, ash, beech and sycamore, poplar and willow. As the forest extended northward it began to include pine, tamarack, and cedar.

It was wild and beautiful, but not very hospitable. Nature is an untidy housekeeper, and the Michigan de Tocqueville saw had lain largely undisturbed since the last Pleistocene glacier 18,000 years previously. It was a tangle of fallen trees, swamps, wild rivers, and cockleburrs. Except on the open water, there were few places to admire a sunset, and a fall color tour was out of the question.

There is risk in going too far in tidying up a howling wilderness. Now we are taking measures to save wild rivers as they dwindle to too few; to set aside forests for those coming after us. There have been excesses of exploitation, and people of Michigan are rousing to the threat.

But it is not too late. Michigan is a fair land, and will continue to be.

— L.C.

The Names
of Michigan

The early settlers of Michigan did not leave many descriptions of paintings of the look of the land as they found it, but there are good clues as to their feelings in the names they placed on their new homes. There was a Mud River, and a few Crooked Lakes, but grubby and homely place names were, and are, few.

Beulah, in the dune country on the Lake Michigan side, was named for Beulah Land, flowing in milk and honey. Eureka — "I have found it!" — shows up three times, in one variation or another. There are nine uses of Pleasant, most of them Pleasant Valley.

There are several Richlands, and 14 communities named Rose Bush, Rose City, and other variations on a pretty flower. Silver Lake was popular, with nine plays on the theme. There was a Sweetland, a Sylvan Lake, and, of course, Willow Run.

A note of asperity was provided by the founding fathers of Yellow Jacket, but Zion was named after the Beautiful City of God. Bellaire was the pretty name chosen by the settlers of the community in Antrim County, and Agate and Alabaster were put on the map by their respective founders. The last two were named after mineral deposits in the area, but they have a pleasant ring.

Bloom was chosen for its fresh quality in a number of places: Bloomingdale, Bloomfield Hills, Blooming Grove, and Blooming Valley.

Hesperia was the neat poetic name chosen by residents of the new community in Oceana County, in Western Michigan. There are seven Crystal Lakes.

Many of the early settlers were French, and Belle (for beautiful) was popular, giving rise to Belle Isle, Belle River, Belleville, and Bellevue, and Belle Harbor. The same sort of thinking must have gone into the naming of the Beau River, in Emmet County.

The local flora and fauna inspired many of the settlers, as might be expected. The names are possibly not as imaginative or flattering as some of the more poetic, but they have a pleasant sound.

Birch figures in four place names, Cedar crops up 21 times, Pine 22 times, Oak in 24 variations. Burr Oak, Butternut, and Hemlock were chosen. Blackberry Ridge, Peach Ridge. Three Evergreens, Fern and two Ferndales. Four Bear Creeks. Fruitland. Fruitport. Eight Beaver Lakes. Bass Lake. Bass Beach. Bass Landing, Basswood, and Basswood Corners, after the tree, of course.

And geography inspired many community fathers. Bay Port has eight variations in Michigan. There are 53 variations on "Lake." There's Limestone.

And then there was brave Sans Souci. Life in early Michigan is not known to have been carefree anywhere.

The Lowlands

Michigan's lowlands stretch from Saginaw and the Thumb on the east to the dune country of Ludington and Pentwater on the west. In much of it, especially along the channel of an ancient glacial river that once transected Michigan from Saginaw Bay to the Grand Rapids area, the elevations are commonly less than 100 feet above Lakes Michigan and Huron. The Saginaw, Maple, and Grand rivers follow the old channel.

Since the visit of Alexis de Tocqueville 150 years ago, the lowlands have been mellowed by time, agriculture, logging, and an encrustation of foundries and factories. Not all of this has been for the better, but not all for the worse, either. The uplands further north are better known for their natural beauty, but the lowlands contain some of the state's greatest treasures in gracious towns and unusual and lovely traces of what Michigan was like before the white man came.

In Calhoun County, toward Lake Michigan, is a tract bounded by a railroad and Helmer Brook that has never known a plow or grazing livestock. It is undisturbed virgin prairie, where still glow pink-plumed Queen-of-the-Prairie, seldom seem any more. And, of course, Indian Tobacco, Queen Anne's Lace, and other more familiar open country growth.

Michigan has its own stand of American Lotus. The last patch in the state is in Monroe County, near Lake Erie and north of Toledo, Ohio. The pale cream lotus blooms appear in early August in the Swan Creek

Estuary near Lake Erie. The place is also home to False Dragonhead, Mallow, and Iris, and is populated by ducks, egrets, and herons.

The construction of Interstate Highway I-94 has deprived travelers of the charms along the old U.S. 12 route from Detroit to Chicago, although the swelling rises of the Irish Hills can be seen on the new route. But old U.S. 12 is still there, a two-laner with much local traffic but still the best vantage from which to take in a section of Michigan rich in history and scenery.

Saline. Jonesville. Coldwater, where a battery of Parrott guns stands still by the courthouse where the artillery company left them after the Civil War. Sturgis. Niles. Three Oaks. It is a land of country churches, Grange halls, and old courthouses standing in their old squares, surrounded by clipped lawns and venerable oaks.

The memorials to the Civil War dead stand with those of the Spanish-American War, World Wars I and II, Korea, and Vietnam, and people still talk about Chickamauga and Gettysburg. Time moves deliberately here, and the old is treasured. The old Livingston County Courthouse in Howell has been restored to its original blue and gold interior, the doors and louvered shutters redone, the oil paintings on the vault doors cleaned. It also received a new heating system and air-conditioning.

Marshall was described some years ago as "an outstanding example of gracious dignity and Greek Revival architecture in America." Still one of the most beautiful homes in Michigan is the old Harold Brooks mansion, fronted by five Ionic columns two stories high that were hauled from Detroit by oxen in 1840. The side streets in nearby Charlotte have not changed much in a century; freshly painted Victorian gingerbread trim, the remnants of an old mill dam, beans bursting from the backyard gardens in the spring, gnarled lilacs in fragrant bloom, porch swings and picket fences.

A century ago the lowland cities grew around dams and mills that ground grain and powered saws and machinery. At Manchester the old mill still grinds chicken and pig feed a half block from the town's main street. The old mill at Hodunk — there really is a town with such a name — did not rest for more than 108 years. It is no longer in use, but the old mill stream is one of the loveliest places in Michigan.

Water was important to Owosso, too, where author James Oliver Curwood built a castle on the banks of the Shiawassee north of the old mill race and pond, a gracious place of drooping willows and tranquil pools. The dam at Grand Rapids, in their center of downtown, recently was bypassed by a fish ladder nationally acclaimed for its sculptural merit.

Weather and soil have much to do with the varying look of the lowlands. The prevailing winds are westerly on the western portion of the lowlands, and the stabilizing influence of Lake Michigan prevents rapid changes in temperature, making Berrien County, in the southwest, ideal for strawberries, and the rest of the Michigan shore excellent for growing peaches, apples, and pears. And, further north in the Traverse City neighborhood is the world's largest center of tart cherries.

The climate is much different further north, where the prevailing wind is northwesterly and not tempered by lake water. Upper Peninsula temperatures range from 108 above to 48 below zero. Subzero weather is rare lower down, and when it comes, it is slow enough setting in to avoid tree damage.

The southeast section of the lowlands, in Lenawee and Monroe counties, is a dark clay loam that is Michigan's closest approach to the fertile lands of Illinois and Iowa. This is corn-hog land, a surprise to those who know best the lighter soils further upstate. Here the precious land is farmed right to the roads, and fences are few. Feeder cattle and hogs are finished off in enclosed feedlots and barns.

North of Detroit, in the area known as the Thumb, lies an entirely different type of soil, but equally rich. It is Brookston loam, a heavy clay soil wringing wet from Lake Huron. An on-shore wind raises the water level in the drainage ditches four feet.

Here the land lies flat as one's palm up through Utica, Bad Axe, and ending at Grindstone City, a unique place where grindstones were once cut from the rock and widely used industrially. The invention of the emery wheel and carborundum ended the city's manufacturing career, but the discarded grinding wheels, often six feet across, still line the old harbor, and the fishing is good.

The heavy wet soil is good for sugar beet culture. The mammoth, gray sugar mills dot the countryside. The Michigan navy bean is a big Thumb crop, as is wheat, the soft variety that is used in pies and pastry.

The lowlands further west are rich in deep mucklands, produced by decaying vegetation in the beds of old lakes and rivers. Michigan has one of the greatest supplies of peat in the United States, a resource as yet untapped but one that may prove important as the energy problem becomes more difficult.

The mucklands are important to growing onions, celery, potatoes, and carrots and root crops of all kinds. One of the most unusual farms in the state is the old Mentha plantation near Kalamazoo that is one of the principal sources in the United States for mint oil. The breeze across the fields on a hot July afternoon is delicious.

The farming of winter wheat in Michigan provides one of the great contributions to the look of things. The wheat is hardy and is usually sowed in the fall. By November the fields are greening into a soft, undulating comforter so lovely and enticing that it is a temptation to roll in, an emerald sweep that goes out to the horizon.

Even after the leaves fall and the sedges brown in the lakes, winter wheat keeps Michigan beautiful.

Upper Tahquamenon Falls

Linden Mill, Linden, Genesee County

Lake of the Clouds, Porcupine Mountains State Park

Snail Shell Bay, Fayette Historic State Park

Renaissance Center, Detroit

Sand Creek and Lake Superior, near Marquette

Old Presque Isle Lighthouse

Grand Hotel, MacKinac Island

Sunset at Porcupine Mountains State Park

St. Stephen's Church, near Silver Lake State Park

Sunset on Lake Superior near Copper Harbor

Lower Tahquamenon Falls

Henry Ford Museum, Detroit

Mackinac Bridge

Copper Harbor on Lake Superior

Point Tawas Lighthouse

Presque Isle River

Bailey Lake on Keweenaw Peninsula

Fayette State Park

Autumn comes to Huron County Farming

Fort Mackinac, Mackinac Island

Conglomerate Falls on the Black River

Mackinaw Point Lighthouse

Eagle Harbor, on Lake Superior

Bond Fall, Upper Peninsula

Greenfield Village, Dearborn

Lake Huron

The "Ghostown" of Fayette and Lake Michigan

Upper Peninsula Fall Colors

McLain State Park Lighthouse

Plant Conservatory, Belle Isle, Detroit

State Capitol Building, Lansing

Fallasburg Covered Bridge, Lowell

Lake Michigan and Sleeping Bear Dunes from Empire Bluffs

Presque Isle Lighthouse

Sunrise over Glen Lake and Sleeping Bear Dunes

The "Suwanee" at Ford's Greenfield Village, Dearborn

The Coming of Fall on the Upper Peninsula

From Copper Peak

Ambassador Bridge, Detroit

Fort Wilkens National Monument

Lake Michigan, Sleeping Bear Dunes Area

Seul Choix Point Lighthouse

Crystal River

Seney Wildlife Refuge

Point Betsie Lighthouse

The Silver River, Upper Peninsula

Sunrise at Muskegon Lake

The Uplands

For many years following the turn of the century, Michigan's uplands, roughly north of a line drawn from Saginaw to Ludington, lay in quiet, following the boisterous days of the lumber harvest that left large areas of the state a wasteland. With some exceptions it became resort country, jumping in summer when the fishing was good, and thronging with red-shirted hunters during the November deer season ritual.

But with the coming of winter's iron season, the tourists departed. Saks Fifth Avenue maintained a swank shop in Petoskey, as did many other firms well known in high fashion circles, but in winter the staff was transferred to a Florida shop that was closed in summer. Cheboygan and Charlevoix, both with a long history of catering to wealthy sportsmen and their families, fell silent, the yachts cradled under canvas on the shore or sailed back to home country.

There was upland activity of a special sort. The limestone quarries at Rogers City and Alpena, on the Lake Huron side, kept going most of the year, the long lakers snaking into port at all hours of the day and night. As the navigation season was extended, they faced 12-foot seas and 45-knot winds to move the stuff to the mills at Detroit and Toledo and Cleveland and Buffalo.

"A mud puddle," said a contemptuous French naval officer who took three destroyers into Lake Huron for refitting in Chicago during

World War I. They never arrived and no trace of them has ever been found. The Great Lakes are moody and dangerous. From the days of The Griffon, lost in the straits of Mackinac early in the history of the Northwest Territory, to the Edmund Fitzgerald, the most recent tragedy, the lakes have been widow and orphan makers. "The widows of the wind," a Detroit newspaperman once described the survivors of lost lakers finishing out lonely lives in the coastal towns.

But even the mighty locks at Sault Ste. Marie, to aid the lakers in transferring from Lake Superior, via Whitefish Bay and St. Mary's River, to Lake Huron 21 feet below, have been closed during the frigid weather of January and February, although attempts to keep ship traffic open 12 months of the year are increasing.

The snow begins arriving in November and by Christmas it lies deep. For years the main highway from Grayling to the Mackinac Bridge was often just a wavering single track where traffic was bumper to bumper a few months previously. And then came the awakening. Snow. Maybe it was good for something, after all.

The land from the Leelanau Peninsula southward was hilly, almost mountainous. Boyne Mountain was one of the first to be developed into a ski resort, and many others followed rapidly. Caberfae. Nub's Nob, Crystal Mountain, Shanty Creek. The Upper Peninsula was ahead of them, however. The ski runs at Iron Mountain and Ishpeming have a long history, dating back to the days when adventurous Finns established the early ski jump records calling for them to leap off the runs and land flat at the end. Ski runs with a downhill landing slope came later. But the Iron Mountain and Ishpeming runs did not come into their own until lower Michigan loaded up on skis and wax, apres-ski attire, car-roof carriers, and snowmobiles, and headed north pell-mell in the depths of winter, the worse the weather the better.

The uplands had been popular for a century as a place to build summer cabins along the lakes and streams. With the coming of ski and snowmobile fever, the more suitable areas have blossomed out in con-

66

dominiums, motels, and year-round homes. The snowmobile has made access to remote cabins and homes easy after many years when it was impossible to get people and supplies in.

The armies of backpackers and cross-country skiers are growing. With one exception, Michigan's uplands are available to any takers all year. The parks are often crammed to capacity. The sale and maintenance of motor homes and campers have become big business.

The exception, and a charming one, is Isle Royale National Park, located off the Keweenaw Peninsula in the extreme northern tip of the state. Here outcroppings of pure copper are still visible, mined by Indians and trappers in the early days for arrow points and hatchets. A National Park service boat is the main access to Isle Royale, but it is a long and cold ride from Houghton, and some travel back and forth by sea plane.

The federal government is working hard to keep Isle Royale a wilderness, to the extent of removing even the rude shelters erected years ago to keep the rain off hikers. There are inns at each end of the island, 26 miles apart, but between them a traveler is limited to whatever resources can be carried on one's back.

But the solitude and beauty are worth it. Birds perch unafraid on the toes of resting hikers, looking them over curiously. The main trail follows the spine of the island, with lovely vistas of forests falling away on either side to the waters of Lake Superior, the largest body of fresh water in the world, and the purest.

The island supports a moose herd, animals who came to the island by swimming over from the Canadian shore. They are no problem except during their rutting season, when it is wise to keep a tree between the hiker and the moose.

There are two small wolf packs on Isle Royale, but they are seldom seen, and then only in the winter when researchers keep track of them by airplane. Purdue University made extensive studies of the wolf population, an activity that has been taken over in recent years by the University of Michigan.

But the season is short. On an August late afternoon one can see one's breath. By Labor Day the toughest backpacker is willing to put away his sleeping bag and alcohol burner and leave the island to the wolves and moose until mid-June of the next year. The two inns are closed up, and the storms take over.

In the early days of Isle Royale an attempt was made to colonize it. A field known as the Daisy Farm marks an ambitious try at agriculture on Isle Royale, and the daisies are still there. But those who tried to winter over on Isle Royale had grim tales to tell the following spring, those of them that survived. Nobody has tried it for many years.

The uplands are home for a majority of the state's Indian population. Peshawbestown is an Indian town located near Traverse City on the Leelanau Peninsula, a land of silver lakes and quiet forests. Near Northwood is the Ottawa Cemetery, where lie buried Indian veterans of the nation's wars from that of 1812 to Korea. There are many Chippewas in the Soo area, and many work at ancient crafts during the summer at St. Ignace. Probably the greatest Indian population, however, is on the Cass Corridor in Detroit, where thousands of Indians are having a difficult time adapting themselves to western ways.

One of Michigan's best-known communities on a national scale is the little town of Pellston, located a few miles south of Mackinaw City, on a sandy area that radiates heat in the winter time so rapidly that it is one of the coldest places in the nation, on a par with a similar geological situation at Sparta, Wisconsin, where a temperature of 53 degrees below zero has been recorded on a number of occasions.

But residents of Pellston, as well as other communities in the uplands, are accustomed to having snow to the eaves and bears walking down the middle of the street. That means the snow birds from Detroit, Lansing, and Grand Rapids will be along soon, putting traffic on the highways and shoppers in the stores.

The uplands are pretty in the summer, mile upon mile of greenery, interspersed with magnificent lakes. Torch and Houghton, the latter

68

named for a Michigan geologist and naturalist who was drowned while making a field trip on Lake Superior in the mid-nineteenth century, are the biggest, but there are hundreds of handsome smaller bodies of open water.

One of the state's loveliest rituals is the annual color tour, when residents from all over the state go north to see the maples and birches in their last burst of flaming splendor before winter sets in. The uplands are the best viewing.

And then comes winter. Travel is through forest and sedge, in calm weather a reverent hush of sleeping nature, in a storm of rushing fury of savage beauty in which the jack pines and poplars moan against the darkling sky and the friendly lights of the next town guide the traveler to sanctuary.

The Highlands

Michigan residents usually consider as high ground the area including the Porcupine Mountains at the western end of the Upper Peninsula, toward the Wisconsin border. Geologically and from a standpoint of scenery, however, a fat strip of land stretching from Hillsdale, near the Ohio border, to Lapeer County, north and west of Detroit, is also highland, ranging from 1,000 to 1,600 feet above sea level and providing ski slopes within easy reach of the thickly populated areas of southeastern Michigan.

The Irish Hills country of Lower Michigan is indeed a lovely area of green folds of land carpeting the hills worn by the glaciers of the Pleistocene era. But for wild, primeval beauty, they do not match the Porcupines, the largest stand of hardwood-hemlock in the United States, a natural laboratory where one is not permitted to fell a tree, throw away a sardine tin, or even pick the flowers.

The Porcupines stretch for 60,000 acres along the Lake Superior shore, named that because from the lake the area resembled a hunched-up porcupine. One of its features is the Escarpment, a frowning wooded ridge that rises to 1,958 feet and is the highest land mass in the northern United States between the Black Hills and the Adirondack Mountains.

Hanging on to the Porcupines has been difficult. Loggers and miners have long coveted the timber and the copper ore locked in their vitals. If the place were ever to be given over to commercial interests, including those who would like to build roads through it, erect motels, and cash in on its beauties, there would be, as a University of Wisconsin naturalist put it: ". . . an end of hardwood wilderness large enough for a day's skiing or hiking without crossing a road . . . an end of cathedral aisles to echo the hermit thrush or to awe the intruder . . . an end of the best schoolroom for foresters to learn what remains to be learned about hardwood forestry. We know little, and understand only a part of what we know."

From the Escarpment one looks down on a genuine mountain tarn, Lake of the Clouds, a glimmering blue expanse of water from which the Carp River emerges to drop 1,000 feet in 14 miles, almost a continuous plunge of wild rapids. Government Peak rises 1,850 feet above sea level, reached by a trail bordered with red elderberries and white-blossomed thimbleberries, rare except in the Porcupines.

The Porcupines are laced with wild rivers: the Big and the Little Carp, Pinkerton Creek, Union River, and Lost Creek. Mirror Lake is correctly named.

The Porcupines are only a few miles from Ontonagon, where the world's largest nugget of free-floating copper was discovered by the early settlers of Michigan. It weighs three tons and was an object of veneration for Indians traveling from Wisconsin to the Soo. They often camped in the wooded dell by a creek where the enigmatic piece of metal had brooded for thousands of years.

It was moved from the site by enterprising men who laid sections of railroad track ahead of it and manhandled the object to the shore of Lake Superior where it was loaded on a boat. The Ontonagon Boulder now reposes in the Smithsonian Institution. When moved to a mineralogical exposition, elaborate precautions are taken to prevent the boulder's being hijacked, an action proposed for years by Upper Peninsula Indians and legislators.

The Keweenaw and Marquette Highlands, which include the Porcupines, and also Isle Royale, are approached by the high country around Cadillac in the Lower Peninsula. Here also the traveler is surrounded by rugged hills with pines stretching to the sky; cold, clear brooks splashing down gravel and rocks to lose themselves in the lakes; wild stretches of timber and swamp known only to deer and badger.

The highest point in Michigan is not the mass of the Escarpment, however, although it is not far distant. To the east and north toward Marquette is Mt. Curwood, in the Huron Mountains, with an altitude of 1,980 feet.

The Upper Peninsula in the highland area is a rugged land exhibiting geologic formations that extend back to the Precambrian period, 570-million years ago, covering 87 per cent of known geologic time.

One of the most interesting evidences of the Cambrian is the Jacobsville sandstone at the approaches to the Keweenaw Peninsula, so ancient that it contains no fossils, predating the formation of life on earth.

It was during that era that the Upper Peninsula was a sea bottom, and a thick layer of sand was deposited. Down the ages this became compressed and indurated into sandstones that are visible in the famous Pictured Rocks National Lakeshore, on Lake Superior north and east of Munising.

The famous outcroppings were objects of superstitious dread to the Indians. Even today, when the sun is reflected on their changing colors above the restless waves of Lake Superior, the Pictured Rocks are an awesome reminder that human life is short and that nature endures.

Another venerable bit of scenery in the area is the plant preserve between Eagle Harbor and Copper Harbor on the northern tip of the Upper Peninsula mainland. On the lake side is a harsh moonscape of puddingstone rocks, rounded pebbles cemented together by intense pressure down through the ages.

But on the sheltered inland side grow some of Michigan's rarest plants, including the butterwort, an explosion of color in the inhospitable cracks and pockets of Dan's Point, where Michigan ends.

The Valleys

Valleys have always had a powerful hold on people's imaginations, celebrated in story and song — "Red River Valley," "How Green Was My Valley," "Down In The Valley" — and rightly so. Valleys bring up mental images of fertile hillsides, cool streams, and civilization.

The valleys were the first homes of man: the Nile, the Euphrates, the Rhone, the Yangtze, the Ganges. From the Detroit River, which is not really a river, the settlements spread along the Saginaw River, the Raisin, the Huron, and, on the western side of the state, the Grand, the Kalamazoo, and the St. Joseph.

The Saginaw basin is one of the largest in Michigan, including four tributaries in the east central area that are rich in history, fertile soil, and prosperous communities: The Tittabawasee, the Shiawassee, Flint, and Cass rivers. It adjoins the Grand River basin and its tranquil streams, a family that extends clear across the state to Lake Michigan; streams with pretty names or exciting ones: the Rogue, the Flat, Maple, Looking Glass, Red Cedar, and Thornapple rivers.

The Shiawassee owes much to James Oliver Curwood, the author of "The Flaming Forest" and many other popular novels, who grew up along its banks and made his home in Owosso, within earshot of its murmurs. He originated a conservation campaign that resulted, eventually, in the old Michigan Stream Pollution Commission embarking on an extensive river cleanup that made it the pleasant stream it is now.

Owosso has had its share of excitement down the years. When the state capitol was moved from Detroit in 1848, Owosso missed becoming the new site by one vote. Lansing, of course, prevailed. Owosso was the boyhood home of Tom Dewey, and for a time had dreams of being the first Michigan city to rear a president. Former President Gerald Ford lived in Grand Rapids, but was born in Omaha. Owosso even won the world's championship in indoor baseball, beating the Chicago Spaldings.

The town was known as Big Rapids when it was settled in 1836, but the present name was adopted in 1875. The name came from Chief Wasso, whose tribe moved from the area to a reservation after the signing of the treaty of 1836.

The Shiawassee flows near Durand, another community that figures large in Michigan history, first as a coal mining center and then for its railroad activity. It was the intersection point of the Detroit and Muskegon branch of the Grand Trunk Western and the Ann Arbor Railroad.

An elephant is buried beside the old tracks, victim of a circus train wreck. Rail traffic is down, now, and the magnificent old depot is not used. But a railroad museum has been developed near it to keep memories of the old days alive.

Corunna, just upstream from Owosso, is an agricultural center and the home of Michigan's only manufacturer of brick. It also is the county seat, and is distinguished for its beautiful old county court house.

And just downstream from Owosso is Chesaning, the home of the famous Chesaning Showboat, an 80-foot craft that toots up to a 6,000-seat riverfront stadium to unload topflight "name" entertainers. Chesaning is Indian for "Big Rock."

Another charming town, down toward the Looking Glass River, is Perry, established in 1850 and named for Oliver Hazard Perry, the victor of the Battle of Lake Erie: "We have met the enemy and they are ours." At that time there were still many in Michigan who remembered the 1813 engagement first-hand.

One of the prettiest spots on the Grand River is at Grand Ledge, a small community just west of Lansing, where the river winds quietly through strata of sandstone and trees that give the place its name, a lovely setting for a straw-hat summer playhouse.

But the Grand is at its most spectacular when it swings north and west in a loop around Grand Rapids and booms south through the heart of the city, directly alongside the Vandenberg Center, scene of a yearly art fair that continues for days, and a successful experiment in city rebuilding.

Grand Rapids is no longer dependent on furniture manufacturing for its prosperity, but is more diversified, an important center for the arts, and famous for its gracious old homes. The Herman Miller Co. is in nearby Zeeland, however, keeping up the area's tradition for manufacturing high-quality furniture. The popular — and expensive — Charles Eames catcher's-mitt chair is produced there, all careful hand work, and contemporary rosewood chests that are becoming collector's items.

Valleys have always been important to wine makers, the slopes leading to the streams well-drained and fertile, as well as sheltered by surrounding hills. In Europe the valleys of the Rhine and the Rhone are celebrated for their bouquets, and in Michigan the activity is centered around Paw Paw, on the Paw Paw River south and west of Kalamazoo.

In addition to standard wines, Fenn Valley specializes in fruit wines from the pears, peaches, plums, strawberries, and cherries that are important crops in Berrien County and other areas along Lake Michigan.

The Paw Paw River is a tributary of the St. Joseph, along with the Dowagiac, Portage, and Coldwater, all streams that wind through lush valleys heavy in harvest time with corn, soy beans, fruit, and garden produce. Back from the freeways they are dreamy, quiet refuges where Holsteins and Brown Swiss graze and anglers cast out their lines.

Further up Lake Michigan the valley of the Pere Marquette is the scene of a wild canoe race yearly down to Ludington, where the Pere Marquette empties into the dune country. The valley of the Au Sable, in northeastern Michigan, is heavily traveled by canoe voyageurs in the summer, but is left to the deer, the otter, and the muskrat when winter closes in.

The valleys of the Upper Peninsula are less accessible, although the Tahquamenon has many visitors every year to inspect its famous falls, and the Two-Hearted River was immortalized by Ernest Hemingway.

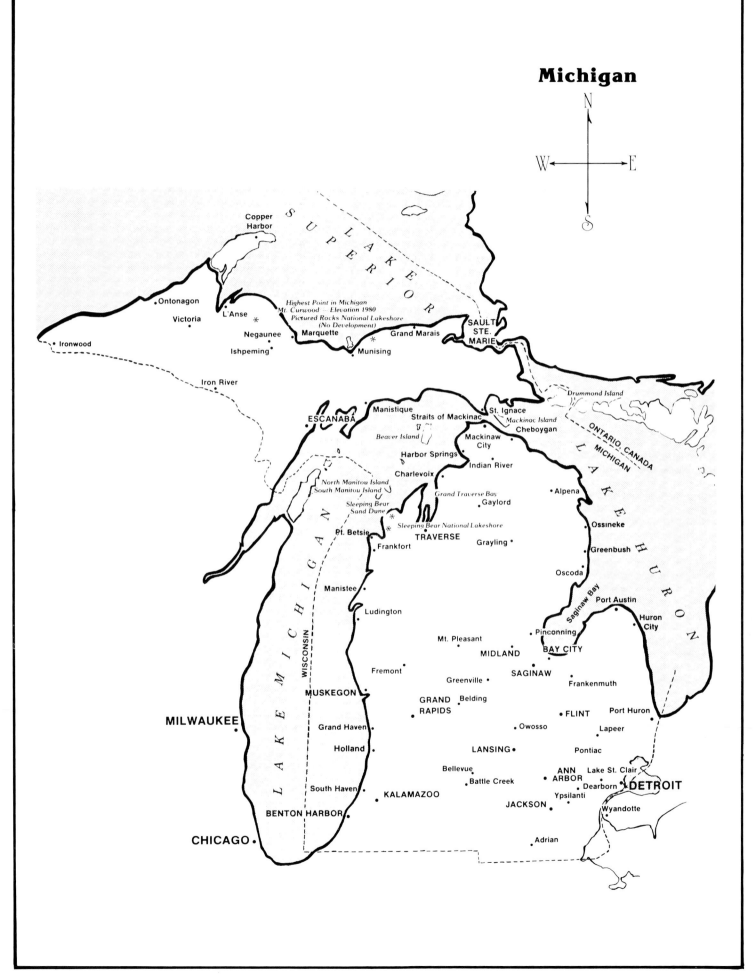

Michigan